Behind the Lions

A Family Guide to The Art Institute of Chicago

Steve F. Danzis

*with contributions by Jean Sousa, Jane H. Clarke,
Mary Erbach, Sarah H. Kennedy, Susan Kuliak, and Daryl Rizzo*

Foreword by Ronne Hartfield

Illustrations by David Lee Csicsko

The Art Institute of Chicago

Table of Contents

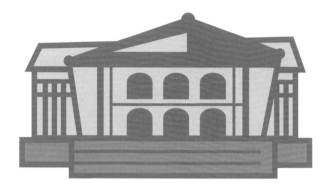

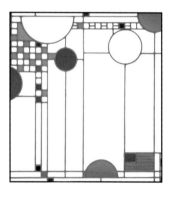

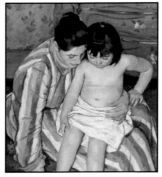

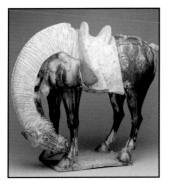

Foreword

What is it about art that engages our minds and emotions? What is it about a painting, for example, that makes us want to know who made it, where and when that person lived, and what he or she was thinking about when taking brush to canvas? What is it about an art museum that draws us back to discover its treasures again and again? *Behind the Lions* was developed to help you explore some of these questions and to encourage you to ask your own. Each year one and one-half million visitors bring us their questions, their ideas, and their interests.

This guide was also created to help you discover new meanings in familiar works of art and to connect with objects that may initially seem puzzling or unusual. While the book includes just a fraction of the Art Institute's collections, the featured works reflect the great variety of the museum's galleries. Within these pages you will find examples of the museum's world-famous Impressionist collection, one-thousand-year-old sculptures from Chinese tombs, masterpieces of American painting, photographs taken on city streets, a beautifully carved ivory tusk from Africa, and much, much more.

With this guide, you can begin your journey into the amazing world of art, a journey that will take you across centuries and continents. At points along the way, you will be introduced to unique objects created by artists from vastly different cultures. The Art Institute of Chicago awaits your inquiry, your imagination, and your abiding pleasure.

Ronne Hartfield
Executive Director
Department of Museum Education

Welcome to the Art Institute

The Art Institute of Chicago is a place of excitement, mystery, and beauty. One of the oldest museums in Chicago, the Art Institute houses objects for everyone to enjoy. Behind the lions are over 225,000 works of art spanning 5,000 years. This *Family Guide* is designed to inform you and your children about works of art from every part of the museum's collections and to encourage your children to look closely and thoughtfully at these treasures. It is also designed to nourish your children's own creativity through fun and challenging art projects.

The opening pages provide tips for enjoyable family visits, followed by a look at the museum's history and the people who make it work. There are twelve chapters, organized, like the museum itself, by collection. Entries on over sixty works have been prepared so that your children can read them alone or with you. We at the Art Institute hope that *Behind the Lions* will make any trip to the museum more rewarding—whether you're here on your first visit or at home planning your next one. We are delighted to help families discover our museum and we hope to see you often.

A Family Trip to the Art Institute

Many families prefer to begin their visit to the Art Institute with a look at the current exhibition in the Kraft Education Center.

Workshops and artist demonstrations are among the offerings at the Kraft Education Center.

Make the Kraft Education Center the first stop on your visit. It's a great place to introduce children to the museum and to decide together what you'd like to see. Ask at the information desk for a Family Programs Calendar to learn what's going on throughout the museum. Within the Kraft Education Center, there are regularly scheduled workshops and artist demonstrations that may be of interest to you and your children. Also be sure to see the current exhibition in the adjoining Hammerman Gallery; these installations feature original works of art, computer games, and other activities in settings designed especially for children.

If you want to explore more of the museum, use this *Family Guide* to help you choose the collections that interest you. Also ask at the information desk for Gallery Games and Family Self-Guides. These pamphlets can take you on art hunts throughout the museum. Remember that you don't need to look at many works of art or stay for a long period of time. Instead, you may find it more stimulating and enjoyable to visit for as little as an hour or two and to get to know only a few works of art on each visit.

Practical Hints for Families

If you're visiting with infants or toddlers: Request a stroller at either the Michigan Avenue or Columbus Drive entrance, or bring your own stroller to Columbus Drive. You may also bring a diaper bag and frontal carrier into the museum. For safety reasons, backpacks are not permitted. If you need a changing table, go to the rest rooms adjacent to the Kraft Education Center or the women's rest room next to the Court Cafeteria. The women's rest room near the Kraft Education Center also has a nursing area.

If you're visiting with children under six: Combine a short visit to the galleries in the Kraft Education Center or to any of the museum's other galleries with story reading in the Family Room. This little library in the Kraft Education Center houses over 1,000 books for young readers and puzzles based on paintings from the museum's collections.

If you're visiting with children ages six to twelve: Combine a visit to the galleries with a Gallery Game. You might pick a theme such as animals, stories, or historical events and explore six to eight works of art.

If you or your children start to feel tired: Look for a bench in the galleries, or curl up with a book in the Family Room.

If you or your children are hungry: Head for the Court Cafeteria near the Columbus Drive entrance. Or consider dining in the museum's elegant Restaurant on the Park, which also has a menu for children. In summer, lunch in the Garden Restaurant in McKinlock Court or bring a picnic to eat in one of the museum's three gardens. You can check your picnic basket at either entrance for a small service charge. All three of the museum's restaurants are equipped with booster chairs and high chairs.

Introduction

7

Visiting a Museum with Children

A trip to an art museum can be a fun and exciting experience. Try some of the following activities to enhance your visit and gradually develop your children's interest in art. If they enjoy the museum, they'll want to return soon.

Explore a subject your children already know something about. Select one of the following topics and ask your children to find examples throughout the museum: animals, familiar and strange; buildings, public and private; the land around us; people at work and play; seasons of the year; times of day; or the weather. Ask your children to describe what they see. Share your own thoughts about the art with them.

Engage your children in a game of "look first, then remember." Ask your children to pick a work of art and look at it closely for about two minutes. Then have them turn around while you ask them questions about the work. Begin with easy questions and gradually become more specific as you test their memory.

Play a game of "twenty questions." Have your children choose a gallery and secretly pick a work of art within it. Then begin to ask your children questions until you discover which work of art they selected.

A Look at the Art Institute's Past

Left: The Art Institute under construction in 1892. Below: In its early days the museum displayed plaster casts of statues instead of original art. This was a common practice in museums in the late 1800s.

The bronze lions standing guard at the Art Institute's main entrance have become a symbol of both the museum and the city of Chicago. Edward Kemeys, a sculptor fascinated with wild animals, made the lions in 1894.

The Art Institute began in 1879 as both a museum and a school. It moved to its present location on Michigan Avenue in 1893, occupying a building that was used during the famous World's Columbian Exposition of 1893 for meetings among scientists, scholars, and religious leaders. Like many of the buildings constructed in Jackson Park for the World's Fair, this building resembles both a Greek temple and an Italian palace. Look for the pediment and columns typical of Greek architecture and highly decorative Roman arches.

Since 1893, many additions have been made to the original U-shaped structure. In 1916, for example, Gunsaulus Hall was built right over the Illinois Central train tracks! Today, the museum galleries cover over 192,000 square feet, the size of four football fields.

Making the Museum Work Today

Over 1,000 staff members and 500 volunteers work to make your visit a memorable experience. Here are only a few of those who work in the galleries and behind the scenes.

Curators

Each of the ten collections in the museum is managed by a curator (from the Latin word *curare*, which means "to take care of"). Curators study the objects in their care, arrange them in the galleries, and find new objects to add to the museum's collections. They also plan special, temporary exhibitions on a particular artist, subject, or period of art.

Guards

Guards keep an eye on every part of the museum so that no harm is done to the art. They also help visitors find where they want to go.

Volunteers

Volunteers do everything from directing visitors and answering their questions to selling museum memberships to helping out "behind the scenes." Volunteers who take school groups through the galleries are called docents (from the Latin word *docere*, which means "to teach").

Conservators

Conservators clean and repair works of art so they can be enjoyed in the future. They also make important discoveries about the history and construction of a work through scientific research. This research can answer questions about how old an object is, what it is made of, and, sometimes, who made it.

Educators

"Looking is not as easy as it looks." Museum educators plan programs for everyone from young children to grandparents to help make looking at art easy, fun, and interesting. The programs can be tours, gallery and computer games, lectures, and performances. Educators also design special exhibitions for children in the Kraft Education Center.

Art Handlers

Art handlers move works of art around the museum, install them in the galleries, and pack them for shipment. They handle the objects very carefully, so that no damage is done to them. Art handlers also keep the art in the galleries and in the storage areas clean.

Questions Children Frequently Ask

What is the largest object in the museum?
The reconstructed Trading Room from the Chicago Stock Exchange building measures 6,050 square feet, making it the largest work by far.

How much do the works of art cost?
No one knows how much a work of art is worth until it comes up for sale. Since it is always expensive to buy a great work of art, the Art Institute treats every piece in its collection as priceless.

What is the smallest object?
The ancient art collection includes several tiny Greek and Roman coins, some smaller than an aspirin.

Can I talk in the galleries?
Please do. Sharing ideas and observations can make your visit more interesting and fun. Sometimes you may also enjoy looking at the art in silence.

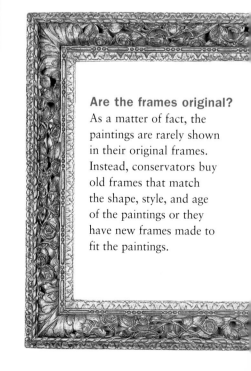

Are the frames original?
As a matter of fact, the paintings are rarely shown in their original frames. Instead, conservators buy old frames that match the shape, style, and age of the paintings or they have new frames made to fit the paintings.

12

Is every object in the museum on display?
No. Only 3 to 5 out of every 100 objects are on view at any time. The rest are kept in storage areas located throughout the museum. Curators and their staff care for these works until they decide to change what's on display.

Is the art real?
Yes. All the objects in the museum are original works of art, not facsimiles or modern copies.

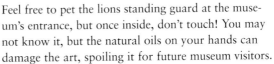

How do you move a 7,000-pound sculpture?
To move this immense sculpture by Lorado Taft, art handlers first carefully padded, and then placed straps around, the object. They then hoisted the sculpture with a gantry—a structure with frames and a pulley—onto a dolly. After it was wheeled to its present location in the Rice Building, the sculpture was lowered into place with the gantry.

Are there any objects I can touch?
Feel free to pet the lions standing guard at the museum's entrance, but once inside, don't touch! You may not know it, but the natural oils on your hands can damage the art, spoiling it for future museum visitors.

African and Amerindian Art

In the galleries of African and Amerindian Art, you'll find objects that were made for practical use or personal adornment. You'll also discover works of art that originally had a religious or political purpose. Look for masks, sculpture, and textiles from Africa and ancient ceramics, sculpture, and metalwork from the Americas in galleries located just beyond the Grand Staircase.

Seated for Centuries

This seated male figure is over fourteen centuries old! Like many clay figures from the state of Veracruz in Mexico (see map on page 17), the sculpture is nearly life-size. It portrays a young man wearing an elaborate headdress, embroidered clothing, and jewelry. His fancy outfit tells us the man was an important ruler, perhaps even a prince. Another sign of the man's high rank is his way of sitting. In ancient Mexico, rulers were portrayed sitting cross-legged with their arms extended. Notice the look of concentration on the man's face. What do you suppose he is thinking about?

The artist who made this figure was a skilled sculptor. Each part of the hollow sculpture—head, arms, legs, and body—was made separately from clay and then was expertly joined. Can you find, for example, the places where the arms were attached?

Figure of a Seated Chieftain, southern Veracruz, Mexico, 250/600.

Fun Fact

Sculptures like this one were often placed on platforms that faced public plazas, much as statues are displayed today.

History Carved in Stone

This coronation stone was carved to honor Motecuhzoma II, the last king of the Aztecs. It was originally displayed in Tenochtitlan, the Aztec capital (now the location of Mexico City). Each image is a symbol of an important date from the Aztec calendar. The Aztecs believed that our universe would go through five "suns," or periods of creation and destruction. The symbols in the corners stand for the first four suns. The X-shaped symbol in the center stands for the last sun, or what was then the present era. Other symbols on the front stand for July 15, 1503, the day Motecuhzoma became king. Eighteen years after this stone was carved, Motecuhzoma's empire was conquered by Hernán Cortés and his Spanish troops.

Coronation Stone of Motecuhzoma II, Mexico; Aztec culture, 1503.

Question

Why do you think the Aztecs chose to record historical events in stone?

Map of Mexico showing ancient and modern sites.

A figure of the earth goddess is carved on each of the stone's four sides. She is shown squatting with arms and legs outspread. Look for her clawed hands and feet. Now try to find a row of teeth and, below it, a pair of eyes. They belong to the goddess's mask, which is turned upside down. A human skull appears below the mask, reminding us that the goddess is linked with the cycle of life and death.

Look Closer

Look for each of the following "suns" starting in the lower right corner and moving counterclockwise: "4 Jaguar," "4 Wind," "4 Rain," and "4 Water."

On the underside of the *Coronation Stone* is this image of a rabbit, which stands for the beginning of creation. Because the stone was meant to be seen face upwards, the rabbit would not have been visible to the Aztecs.

Animal Powers

The *chiwara* dance headdresses shown below were made and used by the Bamana people, who farm the dry grasslands of central Mali. Dancers in fiber costumes wear headdresses like these in ceremonies held just before planting season. Each headdress includes features of two animals: the antelope and the anteater. Bamana farmers admire the anteater because its narrow snout allows it to dig into hard, dry ground. They also admire the grace and stamina of the antelope, suggested here by a triangular mane and long horns. The Bamana hope that the ceremonies will inspire *chiwara*—a mythical creature said to have taught the Bamana how to farm— to grant them a good harvest.

What animals do you associate with farming? Why?

Map of Africa.

Pair of Headdresses (chiwara kunw), Ségou, Mali; Bamana, mid-19th/ early-20th century.

A Woman of Strength

A Senufo artist from West Africa made this drum from wood and animal hide. Instead of resting on a simple base, the drum is balanced on the head of a seated woman. This unusual feature may have been inspired by a ceremony in which men play drums held up by women. It may also have been inspired by the way Senufo women carry heavy loads on their heads. The seated woman supports the drum with long, upraised arms. In Senufo society, women play important roles; this is reflected in the strength and dignity of this sculpted figure. Look on the side of the drum for a crocodile, a warrior, and a snake with a fish in its mouth. These images have symbolic meaning for the Senufo.

Look Closer

Notice that the headdress on the left includes a young offspring. This headdress suggests the importance of fertility of all kinds.

Ceremonial Drum (pliéwo), Côte D'Ivoire (Ivory Coast); Senufo, 1930/50.

African and Amerindian Art

Ivory for an Altar

This ivory elephant tusk comes from the Kingdom of Benin in Nigeria, which is home to the Edo people. The tusk was carved in the mid-19th century for Oba Adolo. According to Edo tradition, the *oba* (king) is descended from divine ancestors. Altar tusks provide a link between the living world and the spiritual world of the ancestors. When an *oba* dies, the son who inherits the throne creates an altar to honor his father. Two ivory tusks symbolizing wealth and purity are mounted on the altar. Ivory also suggests the strength, longevity, and wisdom of the elephant. Carvings on each tusk tell stories of great *obas* from the past, whose spirits continue to protect the Edo people.

Royal Altar Tusk, Kingdom of Benin, Nigeria; Edo, mid-19th century.

His Royal Majesty Oba Erediauwa wears a garment made of coral beads for the celebration of *Igue*. This annual set of ceremonies is meant to strengthen the *oba* and his kingdom.

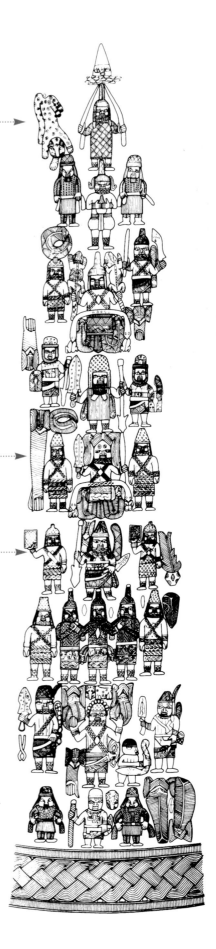

The Pouncing Leopard

Every *oba* is praised as *Ekpe-n'Owa*, "leopard of the world," and as *Ekpelobo*, "pouncing leopard who never misses his prey."

Question

Can you find a pair of crocodiles in this drawing? The Edo believe that crocodiles patrol important seaports and rivers for Olokun, god of the sea.

The *Oba*'s Trunk-Hand

An elephant's head with the trunk ending in a fist is a symbol of the *oba*'s ancestors. This fist represents the great strength of the Kingdom of Benin.

Ekpate

The *ekpate* are female spiritual guardians who accompany and protect the *oba* during public appearances.

Drawing of the *Royal Altar Tusk*.

A Spirit Mask

Mask (mukenga), Kasai region,
Democratic Republic of Congo;
Kuba, late-19th/mid-20th century.

A *mukenga* mask worn at a funeral held
in the village of Bushoong in the Democratic
Republic of Congo (see map on page 18).

Masks play a large role in ceremonies of the Kuba people. This mask was worn by dancers in rituals honoring important individuals such as kings. A Kuba artist used different materials and animal features to portray a powerful nature spirit. Two bells represent the chameleon's all-seeing eyes, which can rotate in any direction. A trunk and tusks suggest the strength of the elephant. The spirit's face is covered by a fierce leopard's spotted fur. His beard is made from the fur of a graceful colobus monkey. These animal features suggest the greatness of the people who were honored in the ceremonies.

Art Activity

Here is your chance to design a mask with the features of animals you admire (see page 22). How will you move while wearing your mask? What kinds of sounds will you make?

Materials: **Construction paper or posterboard strips; fabric scraps, feathers, foil, paper streamers, tissue paper, yarn, or any other interesting materials you can find**

Tools: **Glue, scissors, stapler, tape**

1 Loop a piece of posterboard around your head. Mark where the ends overlap to fit snugly. Take the board off your head and staple the ends together. Make sure the smooth side of the staple rests against your head.

2 Staple a long piece of poster-board at a right angle to the head-band. Loop the piece over and staple it to the other side of the headband.

3 Make animal features out of the materials you have found. Glue or tape the features to the mask.

American Arts

From its first days, the United States has had its own rich artistic traditions. In the American Arts galleries in the Rice Building, you'll find paintings and sculpture from 1720 to 1900. You'll also discover furniture, silver, and other decorative objects, some of them created by unknown artists. The collection also holds important paintings by famous American artists of the nineteenth century, such as Mary Cassatt, James McNeill Whistler, and Winslow Homer.

Proud in Defeat

Look Closer

Hosmer sculpted Zenobia in a toga, the most common garment in ancient Rome. What else do you notice about the Queen?

Harriet Hosmer (American, 1830–1908), *Zenobia, Queen of Palmyra*, c. 1857.

Queen Zenobia ruled over Palmyra, a province of the Roman Empire located in what is now Syria. Not content with her lands, she conquered Egypt and much of Asia Minor before being defeated in 272 by the Roman Emperor Aurelian, who forced her to march in chains through Rome. When Harriet Hosmer created this marble sculpture, she said she wanted to show that Zenobia was "calm, grand, and strong within herself." What do you think the pose suggests about Zenobia's feelings?

An independent spirit herself, Hosmer was among the first American female sculptors to work in marble. She was drawn toward female subjects who, like her, challenged traditional ideas about the roles that women can fulfill in life.

Struggle against the Sea

Winslow Homer spent many summers painting in Maine, and in 1883 he bought a home there overlooking the Atlantic. He sometimes waited days or even months to get the effect of light on water that he wanted for a painting. "You must wait and wait patiently," he said, "until the exceptional, the wonderful effect or aspect comes."

As he worked one morning, Homer saw a fishing fleet following a school of herring. He used the sketches he made that day for *The Herring Net*. The painting shows two fishermen in a small boat that was launched from one of the larger fishing boats in the background. One of the fishermen hauls in a net full of glistening herring

Winslow Homer (American, 1836–1910), *Netting the Fish,* **date unknown.**

Compare *Netting the Fish* to *The Herring Net.* How would you describe the differences between these two works of art about fishing?

Winslow Homer,
***The Herring Net,* 1885.**

while the other, a boy, unloads the catch. Although the larger boats can be seen in the misty background, the fishermen seem isolated and vulnerable as they try to keep the boat steady.

Look closely at the painting. What other details did Homer include to help us see and feel the struggle of the fishermen against the sea?

Fun Fact

In order to make sketches for this scene, Homer hired a local boy to row him out to the fishing fleet.

Ready for Takeoff

The sculptor John Bellamy loved carving eagles. He created eagle figureheads for ships, ornamental eagles for homes and public buildings, and furniture decorated with eagles. Given what you know about eagles, why do you think Bellamy favored them?

Bellamy's carvings vary in size and position, but they all share his unique style. He gave the eagle a simple shape, emphasizing its fierce and graceful nature. The carving shown here is typical of his work. An eagle crouches with its wings spread open, preparing to fly off. Most of the bird is carved out of one piece of wood about an inch thick. Another piece, placed over the first one, portrays the neck and head. Below the eagle are two American flags and a shield.

John Haley Bellamy
(American, 1836–1914), *Eagle*, 1870/1900.

Question

Compare the photograph at right with Bellamy's sculpture. Do you think the artist captured the spirit of an eagle in his work?

Photograph of a bald eagle.

Patriotism in Action

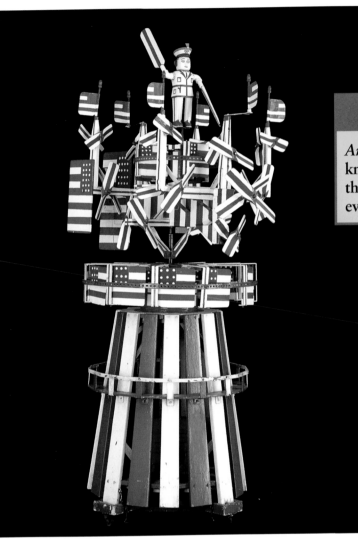

Frank Memkus (American, 1895–1965), Whirligig, entitled *America*, 1938/42.

American Arts

A strong breeze will set this six-foot-tall whirligig in motion. Plane propellers turn, flags flutter, and a seaman proudly salutes. But the only real function of this piece is to amuse people. Spinning toys called whirligigs have been around for hundreds of years. *America* was created during World War II by Frank Memkus, a Lithuanian immi-grant. The artist wanted to express his feelings of patriotism in those troubled times. He brought the whirligig outdoors on special occa-sions, like the Fourth of July.

When you visit the American Arts galleries, find this work and see if you can count the number of American flags. Then try counting all of *America*'s different parts.

A Tender Moment

Mary Cassatt often painted women and children. Here, from a high angle, we see a woman tenderly bathing a little girl using a wash basin and a pitcher of water. *The Bath* was painted over a hundred years ago, when many homes still lacked running water and separate rooms for bathing. Both the woman and child are focused on their simple task. The stripes in the woman's dress and the other patterns in the room help draw our attention to the child's pale skin.

Notice that the water pitcher is cut off at the bottom. Cassatt was influenced by Japanese prints, which often contain striking patterns and objects cut off by the picture frame.

Question

How many different patterns can you find in *The Bath*?

Mary Cassatt
(American, 1844–1926),
The Bath, 1891–92.

Art Activity

Make a patriotic pinwheel inspired by the whirligig on page 29. Then gently blow on your pinwheel and watch it spin.

Materials: 6" square piece of paper, pencil, pushpin or thumbtack

Tools: Pencil, red and blue markers, ruler, scissors

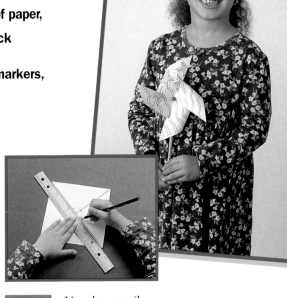

1 Use the markers to create a patriotic design on the paper. Include red, white, and blue stars, stripes, and other patriotic shapes.

2 Use the pencil and ruler to draw an X on the other side of the paper. Mark off ½" on each of the four lines that fan out from the center X.

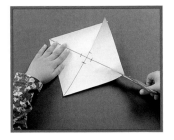

3 Cut along the lines from the outside edge to the center, being careful to stop at the points you have marked off.

4 Turn the paper over. Make a small dot on every other flap of the square. Fold the marked points to the center and glue them down.

5 Ask a grown-up to help you poke a pushpin or thumbtack through all the layers of paper and into the eraser end of the pencil.

Ancient Art

In the galleries east of McKinlock Court, you will see works of art long buried in tombs or found in the ruins of ancient cities. Look for coins, earthenware jars, and glass vessels from Greece and Italy. Then try to find carved reliefs and other works of sculpture that can tell you what life was like in Egypt thousands of years ago. To learn more about these ancient treasures, explore the multimedia guide called *Cleopatra*, which can be found next to the Ancient Art galleries.

Stories in Pottery

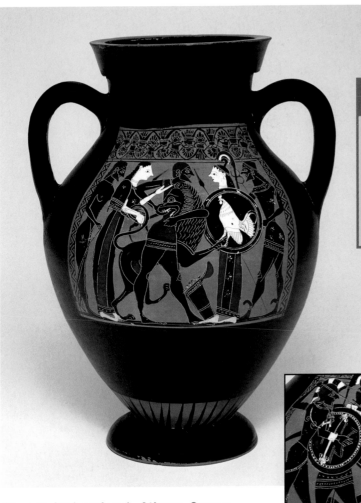

Detail of the back of the *Storage Jar.*

Storage Jar (amphora), Athens, Greece, The Painter of Tarquinia RC 3984, 550/525 B.C.

In ancient Greece, artists painted scenes from Greek myths on the surface of jars. The front of this storage jar, or *amphora*, shows Hercules, a famous hero, strangling a fierce lion. Next to him is Athena, the goddess of war, who carries a shield and spear. On the far right stands Hermes, the messenger of the gods.

The back of the jar shows four warriors fighting over the body and armor of a fallen soldier. This amphora may have been used to store wine or olives, or it may have been given as a prize for victory at the Panathenaic Games. Held every four years in Athens, this competition was the forerunner of our modern Olympic Games.

Life after Death

For the ancient Egyptians, life on earth was only a beginning. They believed that after death they would journey to another world called the "afterlife." Since people would still need their bodies in the next world, they arranged to have them carefully preserved. Corpses were made into mummies by drying them out and wrapping them in cloth. Many mummies have remained intact for thousands of years. On the right is a case holding the body of a man who lived 2,900 years ago! The Egyptians stocked tombs with items for the dead to use in the afterlife, such as food, clothing, and furniture. They even placed statues of servants in the tombs of wealthy people to work for them in the afterlife.

Fun Fact

Making a mummy could be a gruesome task. For example, the dead person's brains had to be pulled out through the nose.

Model Boat, **Egypt, Middle Kingdom, Dynasty 11/12 (c. 2134–1784 B.C.)**

Boats were the most important means of transportation in ancient Egypt. The model boat shown below, complete with its crew, was placed in an Egyptian tomb so that the person buried there would have transportation in the afterlife.

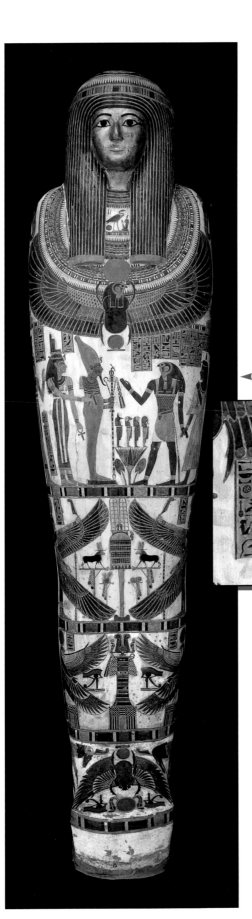

Mummy Case of Paankhenamun,
Egypt, Third Intermediate Period,
Dynasty 22 (c. 945–715 B.C.)

Paankhenamun's mummy case has pictures of gods who will help him enter the afterlife: Horus, a hawk-headed god, is shown leading Paankhenamun into the afterlife. Osiris, the ruler of the dead, is wrapped like a mummy. Isis, the sister and wife of Osiris, holds in her hand an ankh, the symbol of life.

Detail of the *Mummy Case of Paankhenamun.*

About 5,000 years ago, the Egyptians invented a form of picture writing called hieroglyphics. Each hieroglyph stands for a sound, word, or idea. For example:

= the *c* sound as in *cat.*
= the word *hotep,* which means offering.
♀ = ankh, the symbol of life.

The hieroglyphs on the mummy case tell us Paankhenamun lived in about the year 900 B.C. and worked as a doorkeeper in a temple.

35

All Hail the Emperor!

Look Closer

Like many pieces of ancient sculpture, this portrait of Hadrian has been damaged. Noses, hands, and whole arms can break off if a marble statue falls over.

Portrait of the Emperor Hadrian, Roman Empire, 2nd century A.D.

The ancient Romans placed portraits of their emperors in cities throughout their vast empire. This marble sculpture is one of many surviving portraits of Emperor Hadrian, who ruled for twenty-one years. Besides being a shrewd political leader, Hadrian was a skillful artist and architect who loved Greek art and culture. He was the first Roman emperor to wear a beard, setting the fashion for most future emperors. Hadrian's beard and curly hair were probably intended to make him look like the Greek philosophers he so admired. He may have also worn the beard to hide a scar.

Front

Back

Coin Showing Emperor Hadrian, Roman Empire (Alexandria, Egypt), A.D. 131.

This coin was minted in Egypt, then a province of the Roman Empire. On the back, Hadrian receives grain from a figure who represents the city of Alexandria, which shipped large amounts of grain to Rome.

Look at a quarter or dime. You'll see a head on one side and a symbol on the other—a design that goes back to ancient times.

Art Activity

Now is your chance to create your own picture language and send secret messages that only your friends can decode. Before beginning, look at the hieroglyphs on page 35 for ideas.

Materials: **Envelope, paper**

Tools: **Colored pencils or markers, pencil, ruler**

1 On a sheet of paper, draw a grid with at least twenty-six spaces (one for each letter of the alphabet).

2 In each space, write one letter and draw a simple picture as its symbol. Make a copy of the code for a friend.

3 Compose a message to the friend using the picture symbols you created and seal it in an envelope decorated with more of the symbols. Be sure to include the copy of the code that you made.

Architecture

The Department of Architecture includes numerous drawings and models, and many fragments of buildings that have been destroyed. It focuses on the work of important Chicago architects, such as Daniel Burnham, Louis H. Sullivan, and Frank Lloyd Wright. Climb the Grand Staircase to see fragments from some of their buildings, or visit the department's adjacent galleries to see their current exhibition.

Light and Color

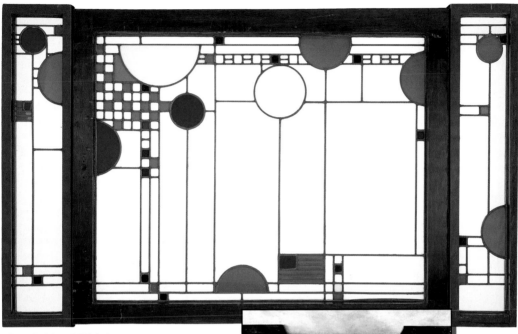

**Frank Lloyd Wright
(American, 1867–1959),** *Window,*
**from a niche in the Avery Coonley
Playhouse, Riverside, Ill., 1912.**

This photograph shows the window in its original location in the schoolhouse.

Frank Lloyd Wright, America's most famous architect, paid enormous attention to details. When he designed a home, he planned every aspect, right down to the windows, furniture, and sometimes even the landscaping. His early style became known as the Prairie style—houses with long, low lines and rooms with few divisions between one another.

Wright designed this window for the Avery Coonley Playhouse, a small schoolhouse on an estate in suburban Chicago. The window created a magical effect inside the schoolhouse. As the sun shone in, beams of colored light would dance around the room.

The window may have been inspired by a parade. Can you find the parade's colorful balloons, flags, and confetti?

The Art of Business

Dankmar Adler and Louis H. Sullivan created an elegant and practical design for the Trading Room of the Chicago Stock Exchange. But the Stock Exchange building was demolished in 1971–72 and replaced by more modern facilities. Fortunately, with the help of a Chicago architect, the Art Institute was able to reconstruct the Trading Room from fragments saved during the demolition. The restored room was opened in April 1977.

When you enter the Trading Room, look for colored art glass on the ceiling. Natural light enters through this glass, highlighting the room's beautiful painted stencils. To create the stencils, Sullivan applied up to fifty-two different colors to canvas that was then glued to the walls. The architect would later speak of his stencils as "color symphonies."

Dankmar Adler (American, 1844–1900) and Louis H. Sullivan (American, 1856–1924), *Trading Room of the Chicago Stock Exchange,* **1893–94.**

◄ ·······································

An air hammer was used to take apart an entrance arch from the Chicago Stock Exchange that was originally located on LaSalle Street.

This is one of fifteen different stencil designs used in the Trading Room. It is composed of fifty-two different colors!

Question

How many colors can you find in this stencil? See text above for correct number.

The LaSalle Street entrance arch was then reconstructed and placed near the Art Institute's east entrance on Columbus Drive.

Image of Autumn

In 1871, the Great Chicago Fire destroyed all but a few buildings in the downtown area, setting off a flurry of new construction. The architect P. B. Wight designed one residence for children orphaned by the fire and another for a businessman whose home had burned down. In his plan for E. W. Blatchford's new house, Wight used a Gothic style that borrowed features from medieval architecture such as carved reliefs and pointed arches.

Among the reliefs Wight designed were four lunettes—ornaments shaped like half-moons—placed over windows on the first floor. Each lunette was inspired by poetry about a different season of the year. What images do you see in the lunette shown below? Which one makes you think of fall?

P. B. Wight (American, 1838–1925), *Lunette Depicting Autumn*, from the E. W. Blatchford House; carved by James Legge, 1875–77.

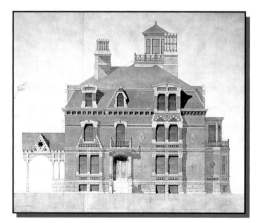

Drawing of the Blatchford House. Look carefully at this drawing and the photograph at right. Can you see differences between Wight's design and how the house actually looked?

Photograph of the Blatchford House, which was torn down in 1929. Try to find two of the lunettes in this picture.

Art Activity

Stencils are used in both fancy public spaces and in the home. Think of the colors in your bedroom. Now create a stencil design on posterboard to hang on the walls there.

Materials: **Construction paper, a 4" x 6" piece of posterboard**

Tools: **Markers, pencil, scissors**

1 Draw a large geometric or simple floral shape on the posterboard. Cut out the shape to create your stencil.

2 Hold the stencil down firmly on the construction paper. Use a marker to trace the outlines of your stencil.

3 Fill in the outlines with color. You might try using different colors for different parts of the stencil.

4 Repeat Step 3 several times to create a pattern on the paper.

Arms and Armor

One of the most popular displays at the Art Institute is the Harding Collection of Arms and Armor. These works were acquired in 1982 from a museum in Chicago that looked just like a castle! Enter Gunsaulus Hall to see shields, swords, staff weapons, and body and horse armor from all over Europe.

Mail Shirt

This mail shirt might look comfortable from a distance, but it weighs about seventeen pounds. Mail is a fabric made of interconnected iron or steel rings. During the Middle Ages, knights wore mail as protection against swords and other weapons. A shirt like this one contains thousands of small rings. Each ring had to be joined to the surrounding ones by hand. The drawing on the right shows an armorer at work on this slow process. Since mail is flexible, it provided little protection against the blows of heavier weapons such as axes. In the late Middle Ages, stronger armor made of metal plates replaced mail.

The Mail Maker, 1425–36.

Mail Shirt, **Western Europe, 16th century.**

Armor for Man and Beast

Armor was worn for several different purposes. Knights put on armor to protect themselves in battle. They also used special armor for competing in sporting events called jousts or tournaments. Horses that carried knights often had their own armor, since the horses were expensive to replace. Sometimes kings and noblemen wore suits of armor just to show off. Their armor was highly decorated, a sign of wealth and rank.

The suit shown here was made more than four hundred years ago. It was part of what is called a garniture, a collection of pieces that could be added or removed, depending on how the armor would be used. Look for the metal piece sticking out from the breastplate. This is where the knight's lance would rest.

James Henry Nixon (born c. 1808),
***The Presentation of the Knights,* from**
***The Eglinton Tournament,* published in 1843.**

Tournaments were revived as late as this one in Scotland in 1839.

Horse Armor
(half-shaffron),
Milan, Italy, 1570/80.

Armor for a horse, such as this *half-shaffron*, was often decorated to match the rider's own armor. Although it looks dangerous, the spike emerging from this headpiece was only included to impress people.

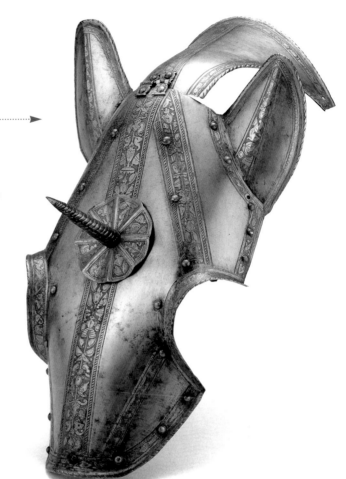

Three-Quarter-Length Suit
of Field Armor, Milan,
Italy, 1570/80.

Question

The suit of armor shown at left weighs over forty-three pounds. How do you think you would feel wearing it?

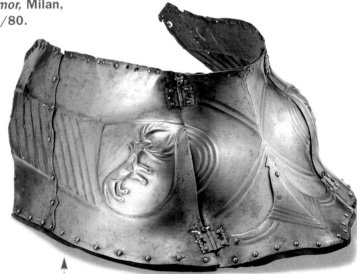

Christian Spor (died 1485), *Horse Armor* (peytral), Mühlau, Austria, 1475/80.

This piece of armor was designed to protect a horse's chest area.

Midwestern Middle Ages

George F. Harding, Jr., thought about shipping a real castle from Europe to Chicago to house his extensive collection of arms and armor. Instead he decided to build his own medieval-style castle. The building included secret stairways and passages, a dungeon, and other features not commonly found in Chicago's homes. More practical was a huge light installed on the tower, so that aviators landing at nearby airfields wouldn't crash into the castle. Harding spent several months each year traveling throughout Europe in search of new pieces for his collection. In 1930, he turned his castle into a museum. It remained open to the public for thirty years before being destroyed to make way for a planned highway.

A view of the "castle" that George F. Harding, Jr., built on Lake Park Avenue by 1927.

Fun Fact

Harding didn't just collect arms and armor. He also owned an Egyptian mummy case and one hundred and fifty walking sticks!

A view of a gallery in the "castle."

Art Activity

During the medieval period, knights carried shields that often featured a family coat of arms— a group of symbols important to a particular family. With some simple materials, you can make a shield that displays your own coat-of-arms design.

Materials: **Posterboard**

Tools: **Markers, masking tape, pencil, scissors**

1 Draw your own shield shape onto a large piece of posterboard. Cut out the shape.

2 Design a coat of arms for your shield and then draw it on the posterboard. You might include pictures that represent your hobbies, members of your family, or your house. Color in your design with markers.

3 Cut a small strip of posterboard. Tape each end of the strip to the back of the shield, leaving enough room for your hand.

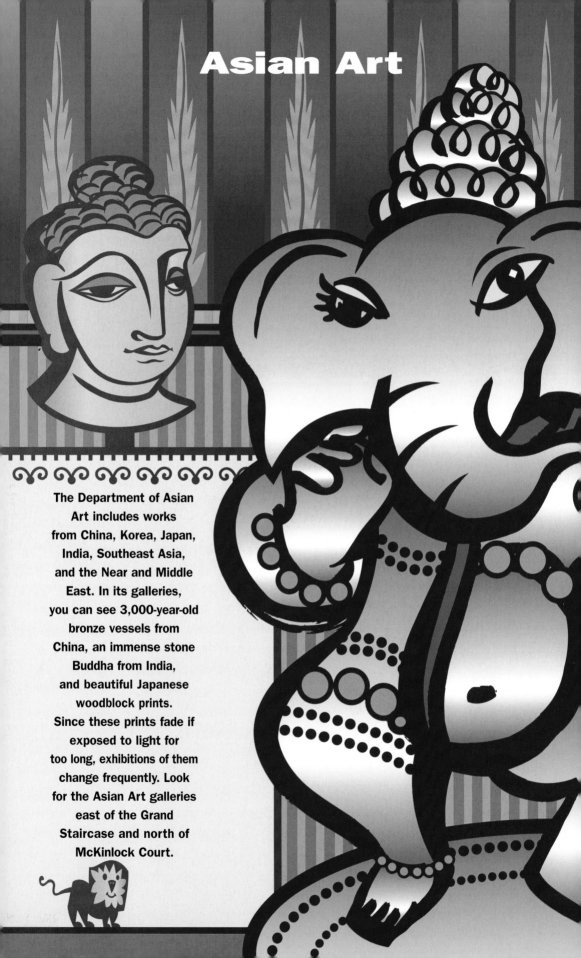

Asian Art

The Department of Asian Art includes works from China, Korea, Japan, India, Southeast Asia, and the Near and Middle East. In its galleries, you can see 3,000-year-old bronze vessels from China, an immense stone Buddha from India, and beautiful Japanese woodblock prints. Since these prints fade if exposed to light for too long, exhibitions of them change frequently. Look for the Asian Art galleries east of the Grand Staircase and north of McKinlock Court.

A Dragon in the Clouds

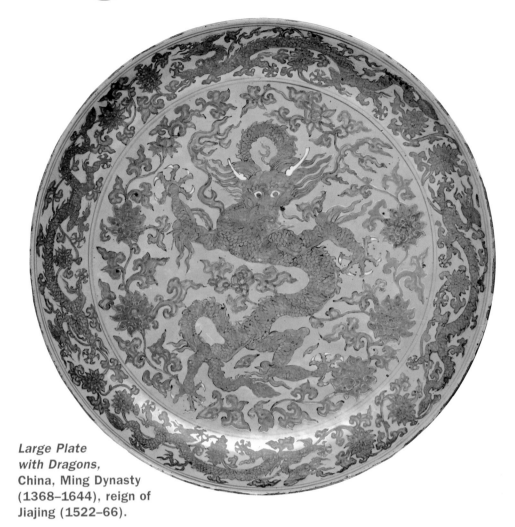

*Large Plate
with Dragons,*
China, Ming Dynasty
(1368–1644), reign of
Jiajing (1522–66).

This porcelain plate was created especially for a Chinese emperor. It contains two imperial symbols: the color yellow and the dragon. In China the emperors were compared to dragons, who could fly between heaven and earth. The central dragon on the plate is surrounded by a swirl of flowers and fluffy, cloudlike forms. Since dragons supposedly brought rain, which makes crops grow,

dragons also symbolized good luck for the Chinese.

Chinese potters invented porcelain, a blend of minerals and clay that form a strong pottery that can appear delicate. Bright colors can be painted on porcelain objects before they are fired, or baked in a kiln. In China, the emperor appointed officials to supervise the crafting of porcelain objects for his palace.

Buried Treasure

During the Tang dynasty, the Chinese believed that the human soul had two parts that separated at death. One entered the spirit world, and the other stayed on earth in a tomb. When wealthy and powerful people died, they were buried with clay objects called *mingqi*. These objects helped ensure the comfort of the soul that stayed on earth.

Sometimes hundreds of *mingqi* were placed in a single tomb. They represented guardians of the tomb or people and animals that had been important to the person buried there. The objects shown here are more than a thousand years old. Despite their beauty, these ceramic sculptures were probably created to be displayed only once—at the funeral procession.

Armored Guardian (Tomb Figure), **China, Tang dynasty (618–907), c. 700.**

This guardian figure was placed in a tomb to ward off evil. In his hands he once held a weapon, now lost. His fancy armor includes a helmet, breast- and backplates, and leggings under a skirt. Compare this armor with the armor on pages 46–47. What differences can you find?

Horse (Tomb Figure), **China, Tang dynasty (618–907), c. 700–750.**

This two-and-one-half-foot-tall Tang horse is among the largest tomb figures ever found. Its size and quality tell us that the person buried in the tomb must have been very important. The more wealth a person had, the larger were the figures placed in his or her tomb. Examine the beautiful glaze on the horse. How many different colors do you see?

Question

If you lived during the Tang dynasty, what objects would you want placed in your tomb?

市川海老藏

Katsukawa Shunshō (Japanese, 1726–1792), *Memorial Portrait of Ichikawa Ebizō II (Danjūrō II) as a Peddler of the Pancea Uirō,* c. 1768–70.

The portrait at left honors the memory of a Kabuki actor. Ebizō II is shown playing a person who sells medicine from door to door. Kabuki was a popular form of drama among middle-class Japanese. The performers, who were all men, used exaggerated gestures and facial expressions to entertain audiences.

Fun Fact

The distance from Edo (now Tokyo) to Kyoto is about the same as the distance from Chicago to St. Louis, Missouri (about 250 miles).

Utagawa Hiroshige (Japanese, 1797–1858), *Distant View of Mount Akiha,* from the series *Fifty-Three Stations on the Tōkaidō,* 1833.

On the Road

About two hundred years ago, Japanese artists began to make color prints that celebrate the ordinary pleasures of life. Many carved wooden blocks were needed to produce a single image. Each block would be inked with a different color, then applied to paper. The finished prints were sold to the public, much as posters are today.

Printmakers often portrayed people in theaters, restaurants, and other places of entertainment. Later, artists turned to landscape as a subject. Utagawa Hiroshige was one of Japan's finest landscape printmakers. His series *Fifty-Three Stations on the Tōkaidō* was inspired by his journey along a highway that runs from Edo (present-day Tokyo) to Kyoto, home of the emperor. Hiroshige captured the pleasure and sometimes the weariness of travel. His prints show travelers from all social classes surrounded by the beautiful Japanese countryside.

Look carefully at the people in the print below. How do you think they feel?

Fearsome Guardian

The *Shūkongō-jin* may look like a monster, but his purpose is to guard against evil. This sculpture once stood in a Buddhist temple in Japan. *Shūkongō-jin*'s third eye in the middle of his forehead helps him tell good from evil. He holds a thunderbolt in his right hand to frighten away evil-doers. Veins stick out of his powerful forearms. With his left hand he makes a gesture that means "watch out" or "beware." Notice how firmly he stands on his rocky perch, even though his hair and clothing are tossed about by strong winds.

Question

Which characteristics do you think made *Shūkongō-jin* an effective guard?

Shūkongō-jin, Japan, Kamakura period (1185–1333).

Dancing Sculpture

This bronze sculpture portrays Shiva, one of the three major gods of the Hindu religion. Hindus believe that Shiva dances on and on to keep the universe in motion. In his upper hands, Shiva holds the flame of destruction and a drum that symbolizes the rhythm of life. Surrounding him is a ring of fire, which represents the essential life forces. His foot stamps out ignorance in the form of a dwarf. Over nine hundred years old, the sculpture gives the appearance of being in constant motion. Indeed, it probably has "danced" in the past. Poles can be placed through holes in the bottom, allowing the sculpture to be carried in religious processions.

Shiva Nataraja,
state of Tamil Nadu, India, Chola dynasty, 10th/11th century.

Fun Fact

Shiva's flowing hair represents the mighty river Ganges in India.

Crowded into a Camel

Seen at a glance, the camel in this miniature painting might not look unusual. But a closer look reveals that the camel is made from dozens of animal and human figures. Such images were popular in Indian art during the Mughal period (1526–1857). The Mughal emperors, who controlled much of India for over two hundred years, were great supporters of the arts. They especially loved miniature paintings, which gave artists an opportunity to show off their delicate brushwork.

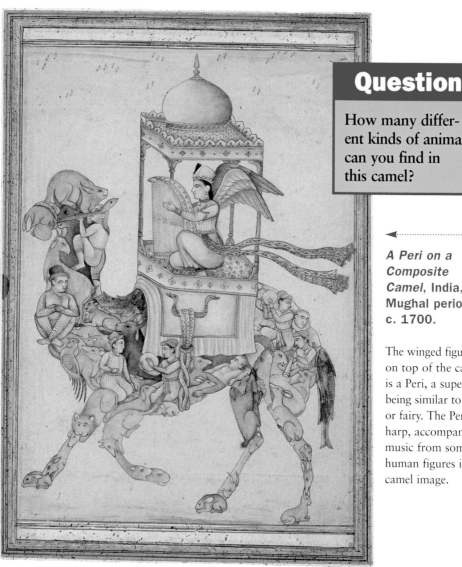

Question

How many different kinds of animals can you find in this camel?

A Peri on a Composite Camel, India, Mughal period, c. 1700.

The winged figure riding on top of the camel is a Peri, a supernatural being similar to an elf or fairy. The Peri plays a harp, accompanied by music from some of the human figures in the camel image.

Art Activity

Study the plate on page 51. Then draw or paint your own decorative paper plate.

Materials: White paperboard plate

Tools: Colored or regular pencil; crayons, markers, and/or water-color paints; paintbrushes

1 Draw a picture in the center of the plate inspired by Chinese art. You might portray a dragon, horse, or armored tomb guardian.

2 Draw a pattern around the picture. Use a combination of decorative elements, such as clouds, leaves, and flowers.

3 Color in your drawing using crayons, markers, and/or water-color paints.

European Decorative Arts and Sculpture

European furniture of all shapes and sizes, as well as ceramics, paperweights, and metalwork, is displayed in Gunsaulus Hall and in the galleries on the lower level of the Rice Building. You can also find sculpture from the Middle Ages through the nineteenth century throughout the museum. To see how furniture and decorative objects were shown off in people's homes, take a tour through the ever popular Thorne Miniature Rooms.

Wondrous Worms

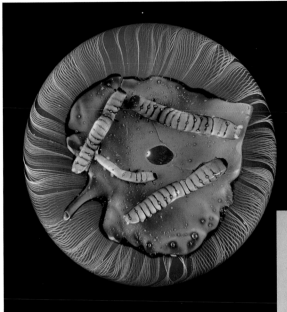

Silkworms, possibly Pantin factory, France, c. 1878.

Profile of *Silkworms.*

Question

If you were making a glass paperweight, what would you put in it?

Chances are you've never seen a work of art celebrating worms. This paperweight features four glass silkworms perched on a leaf that looks as if it had been partially eaten. Notice the strands of glass surrounding the leaf, which resemble silk strands. The paperweight was probably made to honor Louis Pasteur (1822–1895), a famous scientist who cured silkworms of a deadly disease. His efforts saved the French silk industry from ruin.

Silkworms is one of over 1,400 glass paperweights in the Art Institute's famous Arthur Rubloff Collection. Glass paperweights became popular in the mid-nineteenth century, when the creation of a reliable mail service led to an increase in letter writing. People wanted an object that would both keep their letters in place and brighten their surroundings.

Gods, Goddesses, and Heroes

During the Renaissance, people became fascinated with the civilizations of ancient Greece and Rome. Artists depicted mythological figures and historical leaders in various adventures. The exterior of this wine cistern (large bowl) celebrates a famous historical scene—Emperor Constantine leading his troops into battle for control of the Roman Empire. After winning, Constantine became the first Roman emperor to convert to the Christian religion. The cistern was filled with cold water and used to chill bottles of wine at feasts. It is made of maiolica, a tin-glazed pottery with colorful images that tell stories. If you had a cistern like this one in your home, what might you put in it?

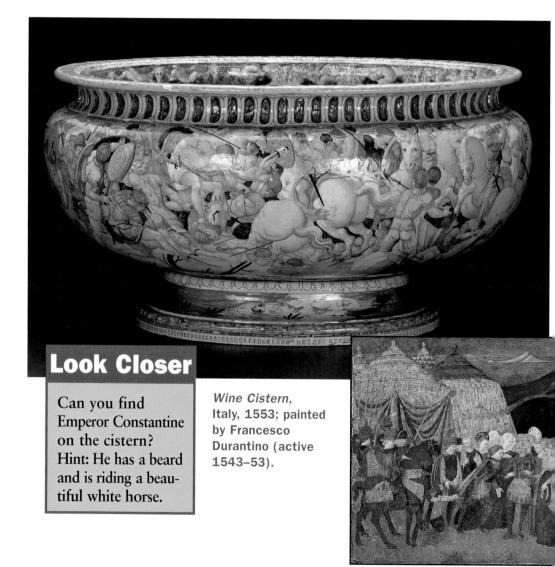

Look Closer

Can you find Emperor Constantine on the cistern? Hint: He has a beard and is riding a beautiful white horse.

Wine Cistern, Italy, 1553; painted by Francesco Durantino (active 1543–53).

Detail of the interior of the *Wine Cistern*.

This detail shows the god of wind, Aeolus, sinking Aeneas's ships. Aeneas was a Trojan hero and the founder of Rome. Imagine what the boats and waves looked like when the cistern was filled with water.

**Workshop of Apollonio di Giovanni (Italian, 1415/1417–1465)
and Marco del Buono Giamberti (Italian, 1403–1489),
The Continence of Scipio, c. 1455.**

Find a wine cistern in this painting of a Renaissance wedding celebration. Hint: It is in front of the stand filled with gold objects. Now think of celebrations you have experienced. How do they compare with this festivity?

Drama in Bronze

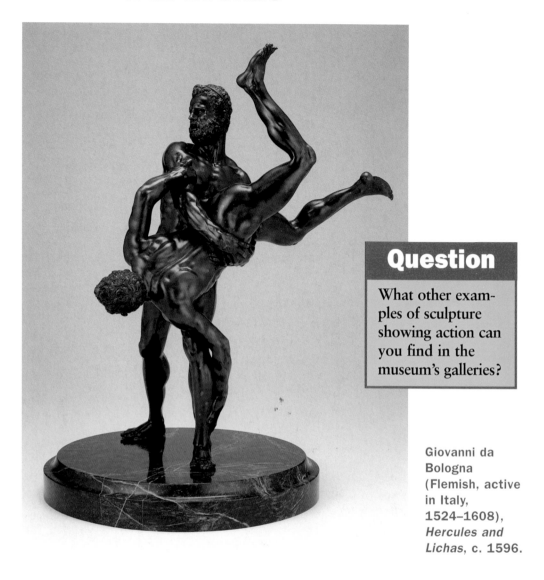

Question

What other examples of sculpture showing action can you find in the museum's galleries?

Giovanni da Bologna (Flemish, active in Italy, 1524–1608), *Hercules and Lichas*, c. 1596.

This bronze statue portrays the mythical Greek hero Hercules hurling Lichas, his messenger, into the sea. Lichas had delivered a tunic to Hercules, not realizing that it was soaked in poison. Hercules went mad from the pain and died shortly afterward.

The statue was based on the work of Giovanni da Bologna, the first European to create what is known as "sculpture in the round." Instead of designing statues to be seen from one side, he wanted viewers to walk around his sculptures and appreciate them from different angles. Find this statue and move around it. How does the work change as your viewpoint changes?

The Allure of Africa

Charles Henri Joseph Cordier (French, 1827–1905), *Bust of an African Woman*, 1851; *Bust of Said Abdullah of the Darfour People*, 1848.

In 1848, Charles Cordier sculpted the bust (head and shoulders) of an African man who had come to his studio in Paris. A few years later the artist created a female African bust. His timing was perfect: slavery had just been abolished throughout French territory, and many Europeans were fascinated with Africa. Encouraged by praise for his work, Cordier traveled to the former French colony of Algeria, where he sculpted people of different races and ethnic groups.

The busts shown here express Cordier's great appreciation for the personal dignity and beauty of his subjects. Notice the finely wrought jewelry the female wears and the beautifully modeled folds of the figures' garments. In his works, Cordier tried to capture contemporary African dress as accurately as possible.

Mini-masterpieces

Between 1937 and 1940, Mrs. James Ward Thorne created sixty-eight miniature rooms, which she later gave to the Art Institute. They help us see how people in Europe and America might have furnished their homes during different historical periods. Traditional Chinese and Japanese rooms are also included in the collection. Mrs. Thorne designed the rooms on a scale of one inch to one foot, then hired master craftsmen to build them.

The miniature Tudor room shown on page 67 is based on great halls in several English mansions. Great halls were the central gathering rooms in these dwellings. Wealthy families would eat meals there and entertain visitors. In the Tudor period, which lasted from 1485 to 1603, the halls were large and comfortable and featured beautiful tapestries and furniture. Hanging on the walls of this miniature hall are tiny portraits of famous people from the Tudor period. Look for a portrait of King Henry VIII above the chair on the far right. The suits of armor next to the fireplace were no longer used in warfare, but they made an impressive decoration.

Mrs. James Ward Thorne (1882–1966) working in her studio in Chicago, 1960.

Detail of the *Georgia Double Parlor* (c. 1850), 1937/40. Below: drawing for the sofa pictured at right.

English Great Hall of the Late Tudor Period (1550–1603), 1937/40.

Question

Imagine you are four inches tall. What would you do in this room?

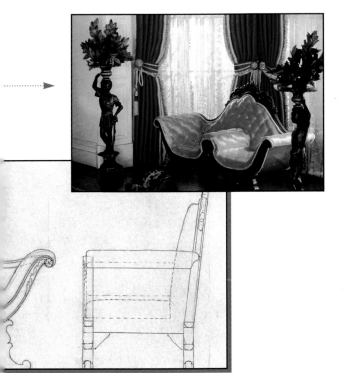

Visitors peer into the *Virginia Dining Room* (c. 1752), 1937/40.

Griffins Galore

Have you ever seen a desk shaped like a musical instrument? This one resembles a lyre, an instrument similar to a harp that was played by the ancient Greeks. At the base of the desk, two carved griffins stare outward. Look for the paw feet at the bottom, which resemble the griffin's paws. The griffin, a mythological creature with the body of a lion and the wings and head of an eagle, has often been used as a decoration on furniture. This fashion was probably inspired by the ancient belief that griffins guard hidden gold. The griffins on this desk may be guarding two hidden drawers.

Secretary Desk, Austria, 1810/12.

Art Activity

Turn a shoe box into a model of a room in your home or of a room you would like to live in. Before beginning, look at the miniature rooms on pages 66 to 67 for ideas.

Materials: Cardboard tubes, fabric scraps, popsicle sticks, posterboard, ribbon, toothpicks, wooden spools, yarn, or any other interesting materials you can find; shoe box

Tools: Glue, markers, masking tape, pencil, scissors

1 Create wallpaper, carpeting, windows, and curtains by drawing on the box or by gluing paper or fabric in place.

2 Use small pieces of posterboard, cardboard tubes, popsicle sticks, toothpicks, and spools to make chair seats, chair backs, table tops, and so forth. Use masking tape or glue to join the pieces.

3 Make cushions for the furniture from small pieces of fabric. Glue or tape the cushions in place.

European Painting

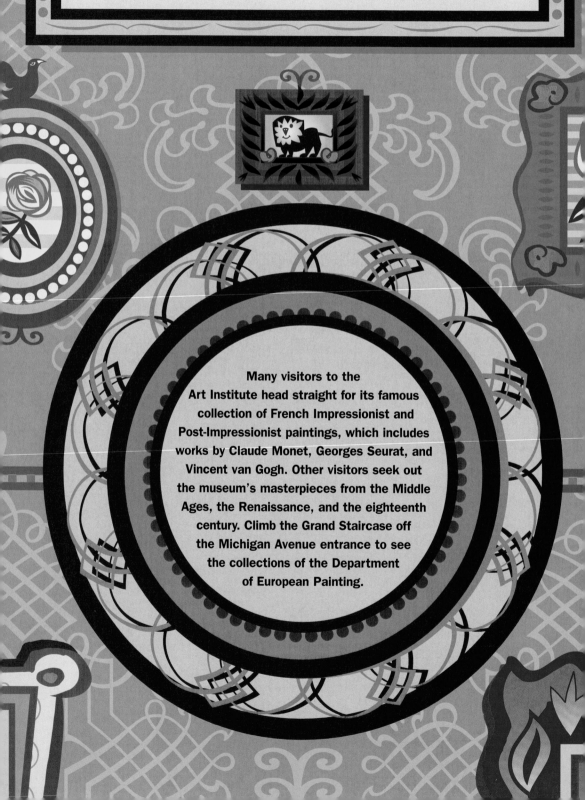

Many visitors to the
Art Institute head straight for its famous
collection of French Impressionist and
Post-Impressionist paintings, which includes
works by Claude Monet, Georges Seurat, and
Vincent van Gogh. Other visitors seek out
the museum's masterpieces from the Middle
Ages, the Renaissance, and the eighteenth
century. Climb the Grand Staircase off
the Michigan Avenue entrance to see
the collections of the Department
of European Painting.

An Illusion of Space

Attributed to
Raffaello Botticini
(Italian, 1477–
c. 1520), *The Adoration
of the Magi*, c. 1495.

The Renaissance was a time of exploration and discovery, but people looked to the past as well as to the future. This *tondo* ("round painting") tells a story, as do most Renaissance paintings. It portrays the Adoration—the story of three wise men, or magi, who come to Bethlehem to worship the Christ child. Christ and Mary are shown greeting the magi on the steps of a building modeled after ancient Greek and Roman ruins.

Notice how the ruins seem to shrink into the distance. During the Renaissance, Italian artists developed an important technique known as linear perspective. They painted buildings and other objects as if on lines that meet at a point in the distance. This technique creates the illusion of three-dimensional space. The place where the lines meet in a painting is called the vanishing point. Can you find the vanishing point here?

A Heroic Adventure

Saint George Killing the Dragon shows the Christian knight about to slay a dragon that has terrorized a kingdom. Strewn under the dragon's wings are the bones of its past victims. Standing nearby are the dragon's intended victims, a sheep and a beautiful princess. The king and his subjects watch from inside the castle. According to ancient legend, Saint George slew the dragon with one blow. The townspeople, who were pagan, then joined the Christian religion.

The painting shows figures in different sizes, according to their importance in the story. Can you think of another reason why the townspeople would appear much smaller than Saint George?

Bernardo Martorell, (Spanish, c. 1400–1452), *Saint George Killing the Dragon*, 1430/35.

During the late Middle Ages, artists used thin sheets of gold to highlight a part of a painting, such as the halo around Saint George's head. Why do you think Martorell chose to emphasize the halo? What else is decorated in gold leaf?

Question

Martorell created his dragon by combining parts from various animals. What animals do you see?

This sketch shows how Martorell's painting may have appeared as part of an altarpiece honoring Saint George. Four smaller paintings from the altarpiece are now in the Musée du Louvre in Paris.

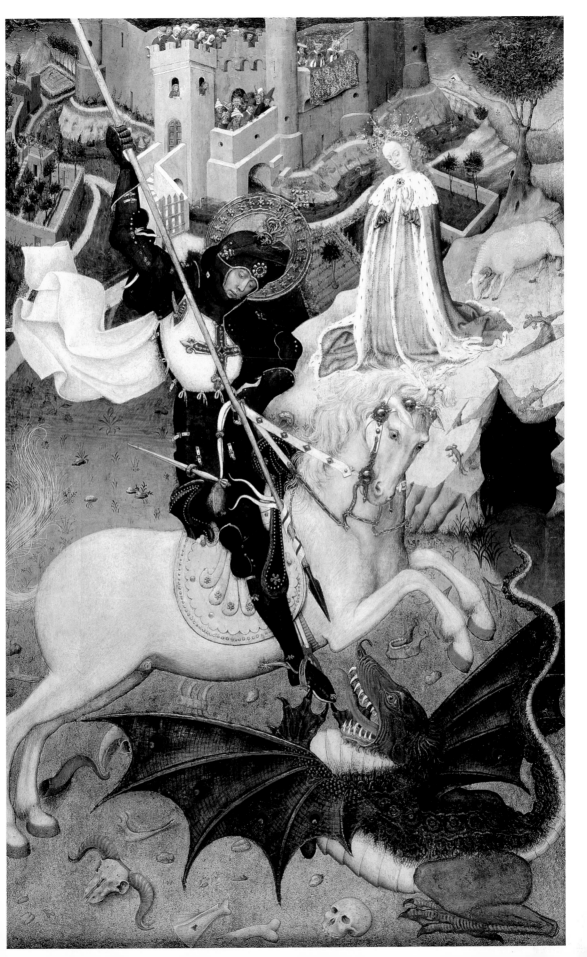

Music and Mischief

Jan Steen (Dutch, 1625/26–1679),
The Family Concert, 1666.

The Family Concert was painted around the same time that Steen made this portrait of himself (now in the Rijksmuseum in Amsterdam). Do you think the man playing the lute above resembles Steen?

The painter Jan Steen is best known for his humorous scenes of daily life. He loved to show people eating, drinking, dancing, or playing music. We can tell from the clothing in this painting that it portrays a wealthy Dutch family from Steen's own time. The man strumming a lute may be Steen himself. He liked to portray himself as a foolish and fun-loving character in his paintings. The other figures may represent members of Steen's family.

Look for the boy pretending to play a cello with a tobacco pipe and the cat and dog who greedily eye a dish of bones. If this painting could come to life, what do you think might happen next?

Child at Play

As an official painter for Spain's king and queen, Francisco Goya y Lucientes designed tapestries (woven wall hangings) to decorate the royal palace. He produced "cartoons"—large oil paintings— that the weavers would copy. These cartoons portray Spanish people of all ages engaged in their favorite activities. One of the last cartoons Goya made, *Boy on a Ram*, shows an elegantly dressed youth urging his mount forward on a bright day.

You are probably more likely to see a person riding a ram in a painting than in real life. Goya painted this animal because he wanted to make a picture about spring, and Aries the ram is the first zodiac sign of that season. What other sign of spring can you find in the painting?

Fun Fact

Goya painted this cartoon in response to the king's request that the artist create light-hearted subjects for the royal dining room.

Francisco Goya y Lucientes (Spanish, 1746–1828), *Boy on a Ram*, 1786/87.

A Moment in Time

Claude Monet was a leader of the Impressionists, a group of French artists who wanted to capture what the eye sees in a quick glance. Monet often worked on several canvases at once, painting the same subject from different angles or at different times of day. This work is one of twelve that the artist made of a busy railroad station. He used loose, quick brush strokes to depict the movement of the crowd and the smoke billowing from the steam engine. Notice how the light changes as it pours through the station's glass roof. To capture such a moment, Monet asked engineers to load the train's engine with coal and send out great puffs of smoke.

Claude Monet (French, 1840–1926), *Arrival of the Normandy Train, Gare Saint-Lazare*, 1877.

Question

What similarities can you find between Monet's notebook sketch and the painting shown above?

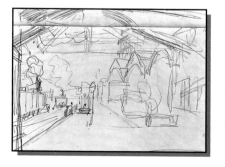

Monet made this sketch of the Gare Saint-Lazare sometime between 1874 and 1877.

Points of Color

Georges Seurat
(French 1859–1891), *A Sunday on
La Grande Jatte—1884*, 1884–86.

The detail shown at right (magnified seven times) illustrates Seurat's use of small dabs of color. Can you find which part of the painting it comes from?

Georges Seurat covered large canvases using just the tip of his paintbrush. Step close to this canvas and you'll see thousands of small brush strokes of color. Step back from it and you'll observe how the strokes blend together to form the people and landscape. By placing differently colored dabs of paint together, Georges Seurat made his paintings sparkle with light. This sun-filled scene shows Parisians relaxing on an island in the middle of the Seine River. See how many relaxing or fun activities you can identify in the painting.

Portraits in Paint

Vincent van Gogh (Dutch, 1853–1890),
The Bedroom, 1889; *Self-Portrait*, 1886/87.

Vincent van Gogh found beauty in unexpected places and things, such as peasant life, a simple chair, or even an old pair of boots. This picture shows van Gogh's bedroom during the time he lived in Arles in southern France. In the work, he tried to express the sense of joy and peace he felt while living there. The room is simply furnished, except for van Gogh's own paintings hanging on the walls. How do the objects and colors in this scene make you feel?

Now take a look at the artist's portrait of himself. Does this painting communicate a different mood? Van Gogh was famous for using color and energetic brush strokes to express his feelings.

Art Activity

Think about your bedroom. What does it say about you? How does the room make you feel? How is it decorated? Now paint a bedroom scene that will tell others something about yourself.

Materials: **Paper**

Tools: **Colored pencils, crayons, markers, and/or watercolor paints; paintbrushes**

1 Draw lines to represent the ceiling, floor, and walls of your bedroom.

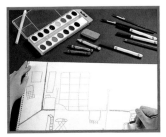

2 Draw the main pieces of furniture and objects that are important to you. You might include, for example, your toys and books.

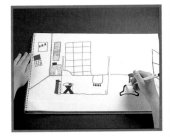

3 Color in your drawing using pencils, crayons, markers, and/or watercolor paints.

Photography

The Art Institute's collection of photography is one of the largest in the world, covering the entire history of the medium since its invention in 1839. Included are works by early pioneers and famous twentieth-century photographers such as Helen Levitt, Henri Cartier-Bresson, Roy DeCarava, and Alfred Stieglitz. Because they are sensitive to light, the photographs on view are frequently changed in the galleries on the lower level of the Allerton Building.

Leafing the Office

We are often told that "the camera never lies." Sandy Skoglund's imaginative photography contradicts this old saying. When she worked at Disneyland as a teenager, Skoglund noticed how people of all ages enjoy fantasy. In the 1970s, she began photographing scenes that she carefully constructs over a period of months. Her scenes are similar to movie sets, but the strange combinations may remind you more of Disney animation than of realistic films. For example, *A Breeze at Work* shows an office painted in cartoonlike colors. Even more startling is the tree branch that cuts across the photograph. Skoglund encourages us to imagine a world without any distinction between indoors and outdoors.

Question

How would you describe what is shown in this photograph?

Photography

Sandy Skoglund
(American, born 1946), *A Breeze at Work*, 1987.

Imagination on View

New York has many famous views, but you won't find them in Helen Levitt's photographs. Nor will you find celebrities. Instead, she focuses on people and neighborhoods that usually go unnoticed. Her work reveals the surprising beauty of life on city streets.

Children are among Levitt's favorite subjects. She admires their playfulness and spontaneity, even with a camera pointed at them. *New York* shows three children dressed up for Halloween.

They pause outside the entrance to their building, like actors preparing to go on stage. Levitt captured them at precisely the moment when they transformed themselves through simple masks and the power of imagination.

Fun Fact

To make *New York*, Levitt used a small, hand-held camera similar to those in use today. In 1939, hand-held cameras were rarely used.

Helen Levitt (American, born 1918), *New York*, 1939.

Up Close and Personal

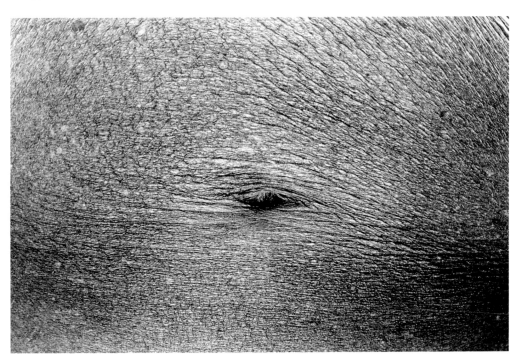

Jed Fielding
(American, born 1953),
Chicago, 1982.

Question

What does this
photograph remind
you of?

Even the most ordinary people look mysterious in Jed Fielding's photographs. Sometimes he shoots them from unusual angles. Or else he brings his camera very close to their bodies, transforming them into strange landscapes. Fielding always asks permission before taking someone's photograph. He wants his subjects to participate in the artistic process: "Their reaction to my presence, the fact that I'm so physically close, makes my pictures look the way they do."

From 1978 to 1982, Fielding took a series of photographs on the lakeshore beaches of Chicago. The picture shown here is a close-up view of an elderly woman's wrinkled stomach.

Private Landscape

Martina Lopez (American, born 1962), *Heirs Come to Pass, 3*, 1991.

In 1986, the year her father died, Martina Lopez looked through some old family snapshots. She was struck by the difference between these images and her memories of the family. She began to combine on a computer figures from these snapshots and from pictures found in thrift stores with her own photographs of landscapes. This process allowed her to create a personal view of the past.

In the photograph above, Lopez included an image of a woman who reminded her of her mother and another of a little girl who reminded her of herself. These images prompted Lopez to think about the differences between her mother's life and her own. Surrounding the figures are trees and scattered branches on bare earth. Lopez believes that her landscapes suggest the journey through life we all must take. She also sees them as a way to preserve memories of people she has known.

Take a careful look at this photograph. Do the figures remind you of anyone in your own family? Does the landscape make you think of a time or place important to you?

Art Activity

To make her pictures, Martina Lopez scans photographs she has taken or found into the computer. She then arranges these images on the computer screen. Here's your chance to make your own version of a Lopez collage.

Materials: Magazines, newspapers, and/or photographs; a piece of posterboard

Tools: Glue, scissors

1 Cut out a background for your collage from a magazine, newspaper, or photograph. Be sure to ask permission first.

2 Cut out pictures of people from magazines, newspapers, and/or photographs.

3 Arrange the pictures on the background you have selected and then glue them down. Make up a title for your collage.

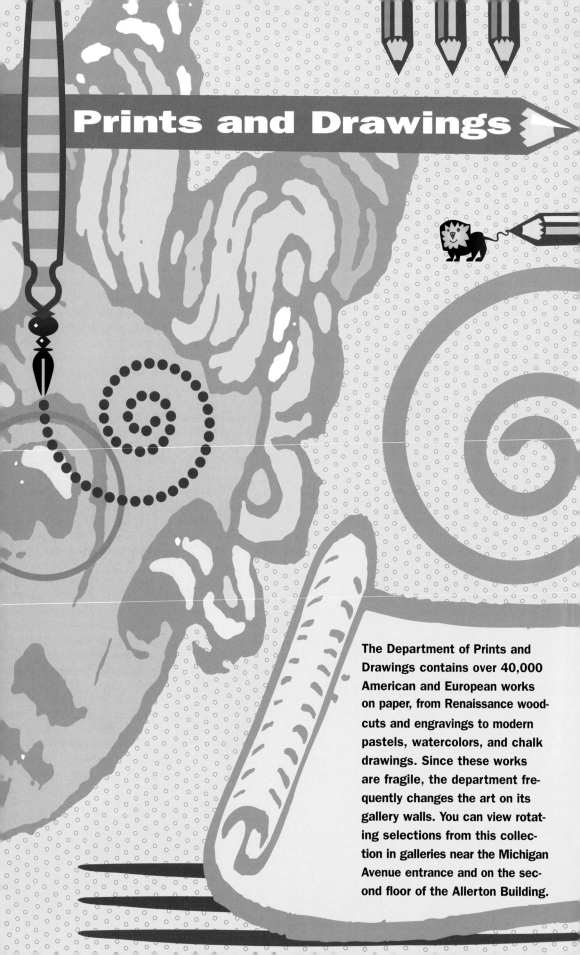

Prints and Drawings

The Department of Prints and Drawings contains over 40,000 American and European works on paper, from Renaissance woodcuts and engravings to modern pastels, watercolors, and chalk drawings. Since these works are fragile, the department frequently changes the art on its gallery walls. You can view rotating selections from this collection in galleries near the Michigan Avenue entrance and on the second floor of the Allerton Building.

Playful Scene

The Venetian artist Giovanni Battista Piazzetta was a wonderful observer of everyday life. In *Giacomo Feeding a Dog*, he captured the playful expression on the face of a boy who holds a twisted roll over a dog. A girl observing them from the side adds a touch of mystery to the scene. Is she amused, or does she disapprove of the boy's teasing? Piazzetta used white chalk to highlight the boy's sleeve, giving it the appearance of motion.

The youths portrayed in the drawing were probably his thirteen-year-old son, Giacomo, and his ten-year-old daughter, Barbara Angiola.

Question

What might the girl in this picture be thinking?

Giovanni Battista Piazzetta
(Italian, 1682–1754), *Giacomo Feeding a Dog*, 1738/39.

At the Circus

As a child, Henri de Toulouse-Lautrec loved watching circus performers. The circus later became an important subject for his art. In 1899 he drew thirty-nine circus scenes over a period of several months. *At the Circus: Work in the Ring* portrays a horse and a female rider galloping around a brightly dressed ringmaster. They are shown from an unusual viewpoint, as if glimpsed by someone sitting in the stands. Toulouse-Lautrec created a fascinating contrast between the large, powerful horse and the slender rider, whose skirt floats in the air. How fast do you think the horse is moving? What in the drawing helps give you this impression?

Henri de Toulouse-Lautrec (French, 1864–1901), *At the Circus: Work in the Ring,* **1899.**

This photograph shows Toulouse-Lautrec at work in his studio around 1890.

Question

Compare *At the Circus* with Renoir's *Acrobats.* How would you describe the differences between these two works of art about the circus?

Pierre Auguste Renoir (French, 1841–1919), *Acrobats at the Cirque Fernando (Francisca and Angelina Wartenberg)*, **1879.**

The young acrobats Francisca and Angelina Wartenberg are shown in a ring at the famous Cirque Fernando in Paris. This circus was a favorite destination for many artists, who loved its lively atmosphere. Look for this painting on the second floor of the Allerton Building.

Life in the Field

Although born and raised in Chicago, Charles White understood the dignity of rural labor. White traveled extensively throughout the South as a young man and was inspired to draw the people he met. In *Harvest Talk*, he portrayed two farmers in a field. One farmer sharpens a scythe, which is used to cut grain or long grass. The other holds his large hands in front of him as he stares off to the side. Because White drew them from a low angle, these powerful figures seem to tower over the viewer.

With your finger, trace the curves of their muscles and the outlines of the swirling clouds and rolling field. Notice how these lines are similar. White wanted the men to look in harmony with their surroundings.

Charles White (American, 1918–1979), *Harvest Talk*, 1953.

Question

Why do you think White chose to title his drawing *Harvest Talk*?

Art Activity

When drawing from life, you must look carefully at your subject. Try to spend as much time looking as you spend drawing. Do the following three exercises to practice your looking and drawing skills.

Materials: **An object to draw, paper**

Tools: **Charcoal pencil or pencil**

1 Draw the outer edges of the object *without* looking at your paper. Try to move your eyes and hand at the same slow rate. Draw using one continuous line. Don't peek at your paper!

2 Draw the entire object this time, not just the outer edges. Look closely at your subject as you draw. Include as many details as you can.

3 Draw the light and shadows that fall across your object. To create the shadows, vary the pressure you place on the pencil. To make very dark shadows, draw lines that go in different directions and cross each other.

Textiles

In the textile galleries, you can see quilts, carpets, woven and printed fabrics, needlework, and lace from around the world. Some of these pieces date back over two thousand years. The department installs three exhibitions each year in its galleries on the lower level of the Rubloff Building. Other works are displayed throughout the museum.

Nations Sewn Together

Theresa Zett Smith (American, 1866–1920), *Bedcover with Cigar- or Tobacco-Box Rectangles*, 1913.

Textiles

In the early part of this century, pieces of fabric called "top sheets" were used to line cigar and tobacco boxes. They had colorful designs or pictures printed on them. People collected top sheets the way we collect baseball cards today. They hung the top sheets in frames or sewed them together to make cushions and other household items. This striking bedcover was fashioned from 108 top sheets.

It was made by Theresa Zett Smith to celebrate the birth of her nephew. She hoped that a bedcover with flags from around the world would appeal to a young boy. Some countries represented by these flags, such as Persia (now Iran) and Bohemia (now a region of the Czech Republic), have changed their names or no longer exist. How many flags do you recognize? What countries do they represent?

All Knotted Up

Royal Crown (ade), Nigeria; Yoruba, late 19th century.

Claire Zeisler may have seen masks similar to this one when she visited Africa in 1967.

Claire Zeisler (American, 1903–1991), *Private Affair I,* **1986.**

Most traditional textile art is meant to be hung on a wall like a painting. Claire Zeisler created works from fiber that stand in open space. "My mission," she said, "was to remove fiber from the wall." Instead of using a loom to weave a piece of art, she would knot, braid, twist, and coil fibers into large structures. *Private Affair I* is a cascade of hemp fibers that stands over ten feet tall and weighs nearly fifteen hundred pounds. The loose strands swirled at the bottom may resemble the fringes on some African masks. Zeisler was influenced by art she saw on a visit to Africa in 1967, as well as by Peruvian textiles and Native American basket weaving. What do you think of when you look at Zeisler's sculpture?

Art Activity

Textiles can be practical as well as decorative. Use the colors from the bedcover on page 93 for inspiration for a woven placemat.

Materials: **An assortment of paper strips, a piece of construction paper**

Tools: **Colored pencils, glue, scissors**

1 Fold the construction paper in half. Cut an even number of slits in the paper. Unfold the paper.

2 Weave the paper strips through the slits in the construction paper. You may want to draw on the strips before you begin.

3 Glue the ends of the paper strips to the construction paper.

Twentieth-Century Painting and Sculpture

As you walk through the galleries of the Department of Twentieth-Century Painting and Sculpture, you can follow the progress of Pablo Picasso, Georgia O'Keeffe, Jackson Pollock, and other artists who shaped the art of our century. To see art from 1900 to 1935, climb the Grand Staircase and walk through Galleries 230–234B and 240–249. To see more modern and contemporary art, wander through Galleries 235–239 on the second floor and then walk down the stairs at the back to Galleries 135–139.

Mother and Child

When Pablo Picasso visited Rome in 1917, he was deeply impressed by the city's ancient art. One year later his first child, Paolo, was born. Both of these events inspired a series of paintings he made between 1921 and 1923 on the theme of mother and child. In this *Mother and Child*, the majestic figures appear to be sculpted in stone. The mother wears a plain gown, much like those carved on classical statues such as the one shown below. On view in the galleries is a fragment of a seated man that was originally included in this painting. Instead of reaching for a fish held by this man, the boy now seems to be reaching for his mother, who gazes tenderly down at him.

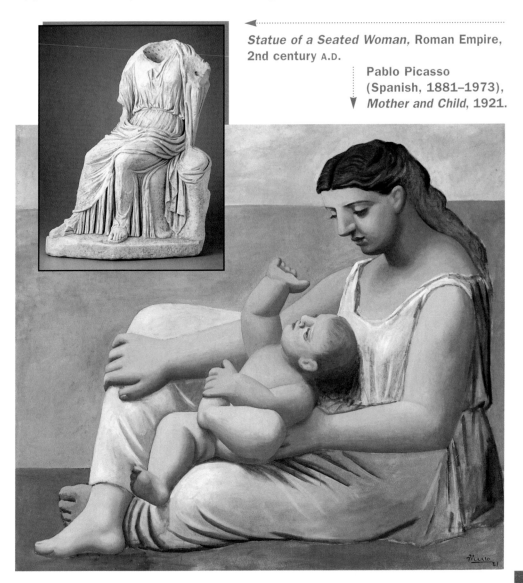

Statue of a Seated Woman, Roman Empire, 2nd century A.D.

Pablo Picasso
(Spanish, 1881–1973),
Mother and Child, 1921.

A Midwestern Classic

Grant Wood (American, 1891–1942), *American Gothic*, 1930.

Many people believe that *American Gothic* pokes fun at the Midwest. Yet according to the artist Grant Wood, a strong respect for rural America led him to create this famous painting. He was inspired by a wooden farmhouse he saw in a small town in Iowa. "I imagined American Gothic people with their faces stretched out long to go with this American Gothic house," Wood said. He used his sister and dentist as models, dressing them in old-fashioned clothing.

Since the 1950s, countless imitations have been made of *American Gothic*. Everyone from American presidents to movie stars to Santa Claus has been pictured in front of the small farmhouse. Today the painting is one of the most recognized in the world.

John Jonik, *Snow Gothic*, 1994.

Question

If you were making a humorous version of this painting, whom would you put in it?

The models for *American Gothic* are shown beside the painting at the Art Institute, in 1942. Though the artist intended the models to be seen as father and unmarried daughter, many people think they look like husband and wife.

The Great Migration

Walter Ellison painted scenes from his own life that tell about a period known as the Great Migration. Between 1910 and 1970, six million African Americans left their homes in the South to seek new opportunities and greater freedom in northern cities. *Train Station* shows a scene in Georgia, where Ellison lived as a boy. In 1936, when he made the painting, Jim Crow laws required separate facilities for whites and blacks in public buildings such as train stations. Separate waiting rooms for the two racial groups can be seen in the left and right sections of the painting. Black passengers board a northbound train headed for Chicago and other cities, while well-dressed white passengers board a southbound train to reach vacation resorts. Chicago was an appealing destination for blacks moving north. The city had an established African American community dating back to before the Civil War. It offered blacks better schools and a chance for more personal freedom than they had in southern towns.

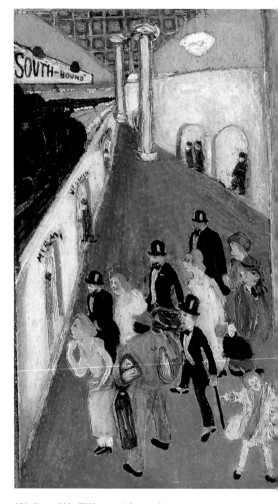

Walter W. Ellison (American, 1899–1977), *Train Station,* **1936.**

Look Closer

Find Walter Ellison's initials on a suitcase held by one of the travellers. Ellison moved to Chicago from Eatonton, Georgia, during the Great Migration.

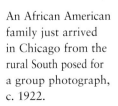

An African American family just arrived in Chicago from the rural South posed for a group photograph, c. 1922.

Dreamscape

Joseph Cornell began his artistic career after seeing Surrealist exhibitions in New York. The Surrealists were a group of artists and writers who experimented with images from dreams and fantasy. At first, Cornell worked on collages—pictures made by gluing various materials on a flat surface. Then he started to fill boxes with objects that he found, such as marbles, stamps, and seashells.

Cornell described these constructions as "poetic theaters or settings." They often suggest childhood memories. In *Soap Bubble Set*, a clay pipe rests below two blue marbles and a white ball, which have the shape of bubbles. The box also contains white coral and a piece of driftwood in a small glass. Take a long look at the objects in the box. Do they make you think of a place or time that is precious to you?

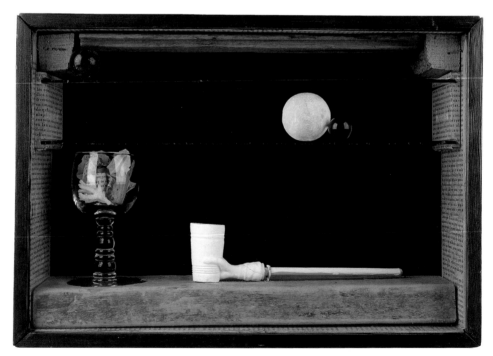

Joseph Cornell (American, 1903–1972),
***Soap Bubble Set*, 1948.**

Joseph Cornell enjoyed talking with children at an exhibition of his works held for "Children Only" in 1972. Cornell's favorite foods—brownies and cola—were served.

Mayan Mythology

Leonora Carrington
(British, born 1917),
Juan Soriano de Lacandón, 1964.

Question

How many different plants and animals can you find in this painting?

Surrealism had a big influence on Leonora Carrington when she studied art in Europe. After moving to Mexico in 1942, she learned about the ancient past of her new homeland. Both of these interests come together in her imaginary portrait of Juan Soriano (born 1920). Carrington presents this Mexican artist as a priest of the Lacandón Indians. The Lacandón, descendants of the ancient Maya, have maintained their traditional beliefs and culture. Soriano is shown perched on a hammock, surrounded by serpents, water lilies, and other plants and animals important to Mayan mythology. Holding a small jaguar figure in one hand, he seems to summon forth the elegant jaguar on the left. Mayan priests supposedly had the power to take on the shape of this magnificent creature.

Splish Splash

Jackson Pollock (American, 1912–1956), *Greyed Rainbow*, 1953.

Jackson Pollock is famous for developing Action Painting, a method of creating abstract images by pouring, dripping, and splashing paint. He worked on huge canvases spread across the floor of his studio. The technique may sound easy, but creating vibrant and controlled paintings this way requires great skill. To make *Greyed Rainbow*, Pollock squeezed thick chunks of paint directly from tubes and squirted paint from a container. This

Hans Namuth, *Jackson Pollock*, 1950.

painting may strike some viewers as a powerful expression of feeling. Other viewers might see a landscape or a scene of destruction in the abstract image. What do you see?

A Pop Parody

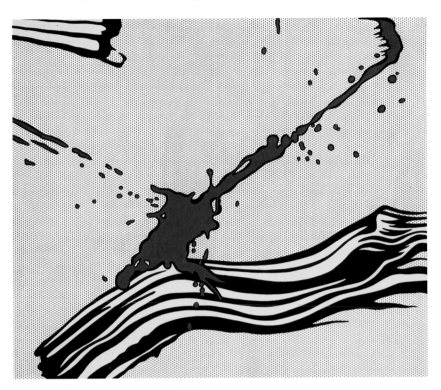

Roy Lichtenstein (American, 1923–1997), *Brushstroke with Spatter*, 1966.

Fun Fact

Pop art has changed what people consider to be art. Some museums even exhibit the work of cartoonists.

Detail of *Brushstroke with Spatter.*

If you looked at comic books or magazine advertisements through a magnifying glass, you would see hundreds of tiny dots like the ones in this painting. Roy Lichtenstein used dots to make his art resemble commercial printing. His work is called "Pop Art" because he often painted images from popular culture, such as cartoon characters, instead of more traditional subjects. If you magnified a section of Jackson Pollock's *Greyed Rainbow*, it might, at first glance, resemble this painting. But Lichtenstein created a parody, or amusing imitation, of Action Painting. His bold brush stroke and spatter look as if they had been reproduced by a machine, not painted by an artist trying to express himself.

Tending the Garden

Chicago's housing projects are often associated with violence and poverty. Yet many of them have the word *garden* in their names. Kerry James Marshall decided to explore this contradiction in a series of paintings. *Many Mansions* shows three young men working in a beautiful garden. Their formal clothing and the "bluebirds of happiness" carrying a banner suggest an ideal world. Looming in the background, however, are the tall, crowded apartment buildings of Stateway Gardens. The painting merges the harsh reality of inner-city life with the hopes of residents working hard to improve their community. Marshall, who grew up in housing projects, wants us to see how humanity can survive and even thrive in the poorest neighborhoods.

This photograph was taken shortly after the construction of Stateway Gardens on Chicago's South Side. It shows some of the older housing that the project replaced in 1958–59.

Kerry James Marshall
(American, born 1955),
Many Mansions, 1994.

Fun Fact

The title of this painting refers to a passage in the Bible. Jesus, describing heaven, says that "in my Father's house there are many mansions."

Industrial Art

David Smith made beautiful art using materials and techniques normally associated with industry. His studio in upstate New York contained a complete machine shop. Smith learned how to weld metal working in an automobile plant and a locomotive factory. During the last four years of his life, he worked on his *Cubi* series— massive sculptures made from stainless steel welded together. *Cubi VII* is a cluster of cubes balanced on a pedestal. Smith polished the cubes to a brilliant shine, then used wire brushes to scratch designs onto the metal. The sculpture is displayed in the Art Institute's north garden. On sunny days, the shimmering surfaces create a dazzling effect.

David Smith (American, 1906–1965), *Cubi VII*, 1963.

What sort of shapes do you see scratched onto the sculpture? Do these shapes remind you of any other artwork discussed in this book?

A family enjoying the Art Institute's north garden.

Art Activity

Choose several small objects to include in a collage box inspired by the art of Joseph Cornell (see page 102). Think about the relationships among these objects. Are their shapes, sizes, and colors similar or different? Where did you find them?

Materials: Candy wrappers, pictures cut from old greeting cards, magazines, newspapers, and postcards, tickets, and other found objects; shoe box

Tools: Glue or glue stick, colored pencils, markers, pencils, scissors

Twentieth-Century Painting and Sculpture

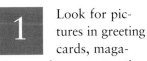

1 Look for pictures in greeting cards, magazines, and newspapers that relate to the objects you have chosen for your box. Cut out the pictures and glue them in the box.

2 Arrange your found objects in the box. Attach them with glue.

3 Make up a poetic title for the box.

List of Illustrations

Publication of this book has been made possible in part by a generous grant from the Julius Frankel Foundation.

There are many people to thank on the staff of the Art Institute for the production of this book. In the Department of Museum Education, we would like to thank Jean Sousa, Jane Clarke, Mary Erbach, Susan Kuliak, and Daryl Rizzo, for their careful and insightful review of the manuscript, Julia Perkins for helping to coordinate photography sessions, and Ronne Hartfield for her unwavering support and enthusiasm. Deputy Director Teri J. Edelstein was also especially supportive of this project. In addition, we are grateful for the cooperation of the Department of Development, including Christine O'Neill, Gregory Cameron, Denise Gardner, Meredith Miller Hayes, and Anneliese Lindeman. We also wish to acknowledge Steve Danzis, for the lively, informative entries that accompany the book's illustrations, designer Mary Grace Quinlan, both for her exceptional eye and for the heroic effort she made on behalf of this project, and David Lee Csicsko for his inspired illustrations. Finally, we extend thanks to all those who participated in the photography sessions: Margherita Andreotti and Bart, David, and Rachel Hirsch; Beverly Baker; Hannah Bonecutter; Alisha, Alphonsa, and Anthony Boyd; Maureen and Patrick Callahan; Alex and Jake Fine; Mary Ann Fischer and Margaret, Nora, Robert, and Sam Sharp; Gabriel, Jandra, Rock, and Xavier Fraire; Alexander Frank; Lolita Gordon, Sheldon McCullough, and Jeffery and Jendayi Ricardo; Michael David Gueringer; Sarah H. Kennedy and Derek and Devin Vaillant; Natasha Wine Miller; Julia Perkins; Kate Perrine; Tara Perry; Mary Grace Quinlan and Patsy Wagner; Jean Marie and John Lake Robbins; Richard Russell; Ria and Rohini Tobaccowala; and Monae Walk.

The Art Institute of Chicago/Publications Department, Robert V. Sharp, Associate Director. Edited by Sarah H. Kennedy. Production by Daniel Frank and Sarah E. Guernsey. Design concept and layouts by Mary Grace Quinlan, Q Designs, Chicago. Typesetting by Z...ART & Graphics, Chicago. Color separations by Professional Graphics, Rockford, Illinois. Printed by CS Graphics, Singapore.

All photography, unless otherwise noted, was produced by the Department of Imaging, Alan B. Newman, Executive Director. Photographs by Mali Anderson, Robert M. Hashimoto, Robert Lifson, and Gregory A. Williams. Additional photographic assistance provided by Annie Morse and Iris Wong.

Photography for art activities by Susan Reich/ Richard Thomas: pp. 23, 31, 37, 43, 49, 59, 69, 79, 85, 91, 95, 109. Additional photography on pp. 6 (top right), 7 (bottom three), 8, 10 (middle), 12 (bottom left), 67, 108: Susan Reich/Richard Thomas; p. 9 (top): J. W. Taylor/Chicago Historical Society; p. 20: Joseph Nevadomsky; p. 22: David A. Binkley; p. 28: Lynn M. Stone/Bruce Coleman Inc.; p. 40: Richard Nickel/Courtesy of the Richard Nickel Committee, Chicago; p. 66: courtesy of the Stuart-Rodgers Portrait Studio; p. 77: Inge Fiedler; p. 88: courtesy of the Musée Toulouse-Lautrec, Albi–Tarn, France; p. 99: Cedar Rapids Museum of Art Archives, Gift of John B. Turner II in memory of Happy Young Turner; p. 101: courtesy of the Chicago Historical Society; p. 102: Denise Hare; p. 106: Clarence W. Hines/Chicago Historical Society. Drawing of the Royal Altar Tusk on p. 21 by Peggy Sanders; maps on pp. 17–18 by Mapping Specialists.

The Art Institute of Chicago wishes to thank the following for permission to reproduce works in this volume: p. 45: Stadtbibliothek Nürnberg (*The Mail Maker*, from *Hausbuch der Mendelschen Zwölfbrüderstiftung*); p. 74: Rijksmuseum, Amsterdam (*Self-Portrait*); p. 76: Musée Marmottan, Paris (*Saint-Lazare Station* [sketch]); p. 81: © 1987 Sandy Skoglund; p. 82: courtesy of the Laurence Miller Gallery; p. 83: Jed Fielding; p. 84: Martina Lopez; p. 90: Heritage Gallery; p. 94: Estate of Claire Zeisler; p. 98: Friends of the American Art Collection, all rights reserved by The Art Institute of Chicago and VAGA, New York; p. 99: © John Jonik from The Cartoon Bank. All rights reserved; pp. 100–101: courtesy of Derek Joshua Beard; p. 102: The Joseph and Robert Cornell Memorial Foundation; p. 103: © 1998 Leonora Carrington / Artists Rights Society (ARS), New York; p. 104: © Hans Namuth Estate, Collection Center for Creative Photography, The University of Arizona; p. 105: © Roy Lichtenstein; pp. 106–107: courtesy of Kerry James Marshall and Koplin Gallery, Los Angeles.

First edition.

Art Institute of Chicago.
  Behind the lions : a family guide to the Art Institute of Chicago/Steve F. Danzis; with contributions by Jean Sousa . . . [et al.]; foreword by Ronne Hartfield; illustrations by David Lee Csicsko.
      p. cm.
  Summary: A family guidebook to the Art Institute of Chicago and the art displayed there, presenting entries on over sixty works from all areas of the museum's collections.
  ISBN: 0-86559-156-3
  1. Art Institute of Chicago—Guidebooks—Juvenile literature. [1. Art Institute of Chicago. 2. Museums. 3. Art appreciation.] I. Danzis, Steve F., 1963–   . II. Sousa, Jean. III. Csicsko, David Lee, ill. IV. Title.
N530.A83   1998
708.173'11—DC21   97-36122
                                                          CIP
                                                          AC